Hot Yoga, Coconut Water and Eustress

10 Strategies for Bringing Intention to Your Leadership Practice

By DeEtta Jones

D0062284

ISBN-13: 978-0615950839 (Shared Pen LLC)

www.DeEttaJones.com

Inside

Introduction

As I ran through O'Hare Airport this morning I heard an all too familiar sound–my stomach rumbling from hunger. This happens to me all the time. I rush my kids out of bed in the morning, grab a cup of coffee, get them off to school (which takes forever with my five year old because he struggles to see me go), stop by the dry cleaner and grocery store, grab another cup of coffee, rummage through the dryer for clothes to pack, pack hurriedly while drinking a cup of coffee and checking email, shower and dress within 20 minutes, and run out of the door to the car, only then realizing that my gas tank is nearly empty and wishing I would have left myself 10 additional minutes. After my plane touches down and as soon as I leave the airport I jump into a car and onto a conference call until I arrive at my client site and then plow ahead with meetings and presentations. A group dinner typically caps off the night, sometimes a reception and then a dinner. By the time I get to my hotel it's 10 pm and I'm physically and emotionally wiped out, but I still have work to do–emails, contracts, design, reading and research.

Yes, I relive this reality weekly. And you know what, it's bad and it's got to stop. Here's why, because this is not how effective and successful leaders structure their lives. It's unsustainable and non-strategic. Effective leaders–of one's personal life or a team of thousands–make strategic choices. Effective leaders are able to step back and see the whole–to view the system rather than simply the thing that is most loudly demanding my attention at this moment.

The whole system includes: personal awareness and positioning; intellectual stimulation and growth; family and social connection; professional aspirations and attainment; emotional and physical health; even meaning and transcendence. This little book is intended help you frame the personal awareness and positioning aspects of your life, in order to more fully inform your personal leadership journey. The title reflects my holistic approach to leadership development. It is written with the assumption that you are committed to making strategic choices about your life's path and leadership trajectory.

This book includes excerpts from some of my most popular blog posts, presentations and other writing, along with new ideas and material. It is meant to stimulate your thinking about each strategy then give you structured guidance on how to incorporate the strategy into your intentional leadership practice. I use the term "leadership practice" as analogous to a yoga practice, or pursuit of excellence in and mastery in any field or area of life. The assumption is that leadership, like yoga, piano, sculpting or healthy living, is something that you: 1) make commitment to, 2) incorporate structured practice into your routine and 3) pursue unwaveringly over time. Some days' performance will be better than others', of course. You are not seeking perfect outcomes all the time, but perfect practice.

As you read, think about times in your life that mirror the hectic scenario presented above and ways in which you might intervene on your own behalf. No one else will do this for you. Leadership is a choice.

Reflection Questions:

What about you? Where is your energy going? Is it strategic—focused on short- and long-term goals? Does the outcome of your effort breathe life into your values?

Leaders don't react to everything. We step back, look at the systems around us and make strategic choices. Strategy requires being just as clear about what we will not do as what we will do, in our personal lives and in our organizations.

Strategy 1:
Find Your Authentic, Multi-Dimensional, Irreplaceable Voice

My kitchen table is spilling over with textbooks, lined paper, construction paper, an empty shoe box, scissors, popsicle sticks, magazines—some old and unwanted mixed in with some of my favorites—a bowl of grapes, several tumblers of water, an iTouch, an iPad, a baseball cap, a hoodie, three # 2 pencils and erasers (and of course eraser dust everywhere). And just a couple of feet away my stove top is covered with pots and pans, field trip notices and soccer equipment slips sit on the kitchen island, and the television silently projects what would be a much more interesting version of the evening news if only the volume could be turned up without distracting the kids. Yep, how's that for a visual? Not too exciting, and not too unlike the kitchens of my friends, colleagues and many others parents of young children.

Add to this that just down the hall is my office with a scene much like the one on the kitchen table, but filled with my stuff—laptop, bills, reference books, iPad, etc. It goes without saying, a lot of us are living pretty complicated, messy, and sometimes downright un-pretty realities. So, why when I look around do I see so many perfect-looking people?

At my son's Kindergarten orientation well-dressed moms and dads walked unhurried through the narrow halls wearing big smiles and carrying the information packet sent to my home the week before bearing a note "Bring to Orientation"; but that I, of course, forgot to bring. "They are perfect," I thought to myself. "What's wrong with me?" Then I inhaled, plastered a fake "cool, calm, collected" smile on my face, patted my son on the head, sat in a pint-sized plastic chair behind a pint-sized desk, and pretended to be perfect as the teacher, in her sing-songy voice, gave an overview of my child's curriculum, behavioral and performance milestones before asking me to commit to being a room mother. I, with the most enthusiastic smile I could muster and a knot in my stomach about the time commitment, printed my name using my neatest penmanship.

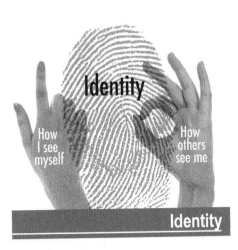

I don't think I'm the only person who does this—strive to create an artificial facade that makes my life look perfect. Many of the women with whom I talk are exhausted, frustrated, resentful, and riddled with guilt. So this is my—and hopefully your—credo going forward: Let's be the modern-day trailblazers. Let's stop striving for perfection but instead for authenticity which includes the stuff that makes our lives' stories rich and that deeply informs our identity.

Framing the exploration of your leadership around the concept of authenticity allows you to bring into play your unique context, and the fundamental elements of your identity. Identity is the combination of how you view yourself and how you are viewed by others. We will talk more about how you are viewed by others as it relates to Strategy #3: Take Control of Your Brand. For now, let's stick to how you see yourself.

Traditionally we have taken a uni-dimensional approach to identity. We tend to think of and describe a person as a woman, outgoing, "a born leader," African American, Gen-Xer, or working mom. Did you notice the "or" in the previous sentence? Odd isn't it? Why not take a more multi-dimensional approach to self-definition, allowing a broader base, a richer context, upon which to build? For example, I am a 40-something biracial woman, first-generation college graduate who now holds multiple degrees. I am an entrepreneur, a wanna-be fashionista, a mother, a life partner, a world traveler. I am an introvert who struggles to make conversation one-on-one but who feels most fully alive when standing in front of an audience. My son and I have "car dance parties" on the way to school each morning, and again after school on the way to piano lesson. I have books piled up beside my bed, a rabbit named "Bugs" and treasure the days that I can practice Bikram yoga, which heals my mind and body. I am a multi-dimensional person and so are you. All of us have many aspects of ourselves that make us uniquely the people we are, and aspire to be. This section is about harnessing you—all of you.

Multi-dimensionality is a simple and powerful concept because it acknowledges and provides access to the unique intersections of our lives' experiences, our talents and aspirations—to help achieve desired results. It's also important to realize that experiences, talents and aspirations may fluctuate over time, with some being more prominent at certain parts of your life than others.

I have experienced this shift in my own life. Before the birth of my son, I didn't associate with being a mom; now it is clearly one of the most important aspects of my identity. Motherhood is a particularly important element of the identity equation for women. This is true even for women who don't have children.

When I conduct focus groups in companies, one of the major points of contention is around the topic of work/life balance. Now, I have to admit, I don't know if work/life balance is even goal given today's intense pace of everything—technology, change, demographics, markets. On the other hand, it is true that people with children (mostly women but some men) are more likely to cite experiences where they: 1) believe they have been passed over for leadership positions, 2) felt torn between a family obligation and the need to be physically present at work, or 3) have suffered repercussions associated with taking "approved" leave to tend to family. On the other hand, there is a recent barrage of articles and blogs posts on the topic of what <u>Marie Claire</u> magazine calls "the newest form of workplace discrimination": a second class of childless women carrying "an undue burden at the office, batting cleanup for their married-with-kids coworkers." In focus group sessions, many of the women in this category describe feeling that work is being "dumped upon" them and further, they are robbed of valuable after-hours time that is rightfully theirs and could be used cultivating a relationship (and potentially, a family). To top it all off, many of the single and/or childless women I have interviewed felt resentful toward women who are married or partnered or have children. They "get tired of hearing about the back-to-back softball games over the weekend" knowing that describing their first date and otherwise restful weekend is considered frivolous; hearing "my husband" this and "my husband" that; "At your age you really should be married. Why don't you stop being so picky?" or the most belittling of all, "Oh, you're single with no kids. You wouldn't *begin* to understand what it's like to be tired!" Of course, the root of all these feelings, and realities—the realities of how company policies are established and how managers set performance expectations—is that we live in a world that is still struggling with a very different workforce than just fifty years ago.

Are you over forty? If yes, what cultural messages were the norms during your childhood? What was the picture of the American family as seen on television? What roles did women play? When I ask this of groups the most common responses are "Leave it to Beaver" and "women in heels" pushing vacuum cleaners around the house or sitting in a typing pool. Just one generation later women are showing up in full force in the workforce, and demanding a seat at the proverbial table. Not only has their presence in the workplace been noted; we are literally changing cultural norms. Think about how the American family and culture as seen on television today. What roles do women play? Is Modern Family in your mind? Or Scandal? When you think of cultural norms, are you considering the expanded role that women play in politics, marketing, media, and their households? The rapid pace of women's changing contribution to society has led to the emergence, in a generation, of a multi-billion dollar industry: childcare. Considering the major shifts that have occurred in such a short period of time, it's no wonder that many companies with their legacy policies that were created with a very different type of employee in mind are now scrambling to reflect the varying needs of our generation, where one size does not fit all. . It's no wonder so many of us feel like we are scrambling, over-stretched and looking for affirm and more satisfying ground upon which to build our futures. With all the changes occurring in such a short period of time, it's no wonder so many of us feel like we are scrambling, over-stretched and looking for affirm and more satisfying ground upon which to build our futures.

Real people in the real world and have sometimes messy, always multidimensional lives. With a little effort, you can pull those dimensions together to put yourself on a thoughtful path. From the perspective of your leadership journey, identity is one of the first major milestones along your path. Why? Because identity sits at the intersection of self-perception and perception by others and effective leaders 1) understand themselves (are self-aware), 2) are aware of how others view them and 3) are able to make needed behavioral adjustments in order to maintain relationships and the ability to influence.

Multi-Dimensional You

My father was one of 18 children in a family from a small Southern town, Marianna, Arkansas. He was a pre-teen when Emmitt Till, a 14-year-old black boy from Chicago who was visiting relatives in Mississippi, was accused of flirting with a white woman. For this crime, Till was abducted in the middle of the night from his great uncle's house and beaten, his eyes gouged out, shot in the head, then tied with barbed wire around his neck to the fan of a cotton gin and thrown in the river. His disfigured body was found a couple of days later.

Iceberg Analogy of Culture

Architecture
Language
Physical
Appearance

Objective Culture
Subjective Culture

Traditions
Customs
Gender Roles
Communication
Patterns
Behavioral
Norms
Values

Till's open-casket funeral was held with the permission of his family to bring the widest possible exposure to this atrocity. Till's mother wanted other mothers to know how Black boys were being treated in the South. My Big Mama saw what was happening and sent two of her sons, those closest in age to Till, to "the North" where they ended up in a suburb northwest of Chicago, Illinois.

My father tells the story of immediately being placed in counseling to help him with the transition and learn how to interact with white people (having never had the experience and with his only psychological models being fear-filled). Through counseling and exposure to a well-to-do Jewish couple, my father turned his fear inside out and came to believe that the thing to fear was being considered black.
My mother was one of ten siblings in a family from Illinois. Her parents are of Ger-

man descent but they identified most closely with their religion, Jehovah's Witnesses. My mother grew up in a poor neighborhood that was heavily black and Puerto Rican. It's no wonder that throughout her adolescent years she always longed for the brown skin and "big personalities" that she associated with black girls, and the black boys who liked them.

Of course, my mother and father met and found in each other some of the characteristics that they had long been socialized to seek out.

I begin my biography—the cornerstone upon which identity is built—with the story of my father, and then my parents, because so much of their childhood and cultural experiences influenced who I am today. Who am I—this brown girl living in a world that doesn't have a neat category for people like me? How do I fit in—in a culture that is built around Christianity and patriotism and of which I am not part of the mainstream? What are my chances of being heard—in a society that largely deems voiceless those who are poor? These questions became staples in my life, and my pursuit to their answers—which necessarily included a close examination of my own and others' identity—became the foundation upon which I built a career.

Much of the focus of my work involves helping people understand culture and its significance personally, societally and in organizational life. Consider the number one complaint clients share with me about perceived weakness in their organization is "lack of communication." Now, there are a whole lot of things that might contribute to lack of communication, but let's start by thinking of this as would a cultural anthropologist.

Imagine culture—sociological or organizational—as analogous to an iceberg. An iceberg can be a huge, solid mass, with approximately 10 percent above the water line and the remaining 90 percent sitting under the waterline. The 10 percent of the iceberg that sits above the waterline is considered "objective". It consists of the artifacts of a culture that can easily been seen, and that also have greatest exposure to the elements—therefore are able to change more readily in response to external conditions. The 90 percent that sits below the waterline is made up of the more "subjective" elements of culture. Remember the last time you went on an international trip, what did you see? What did you smell? What did you eat? How were people dressed? These are the "above the waterline" aspects of culture. Did you participate in any traditional celebrations? If yes, the visible aspects—the food, clothes, songs, etc.—were the "above the waterline" aspects of the culture. The "below the waterline" aspects of the same celebration would include the historical significance and symbolism involved with the performance of rituals. The deeper meaning that is filled with nuance and rich historical context is 90 percent of all cultures' reality. These are also the elements, like an iceberg, that are most deeply embedded and are less apt to quickly changing in response to environmental shifts. In essence, the "below the waterline" parts of culture are the strongest, most deeply embedded portions that guide "how things really work around here."

Now, let's get back to communication. "Above the waterline" of an organization's culture you will likely see things like an organization chart with reporting lines, or a values statement that references open communication, timely feedback and accountability, or a manager's open door policy. Below the waterline are the more subtle and typically undocumented "rules" about communication; the norms, if you will.

Most U.S. institutions, from schools to corporations, practice what cultural anthropologist Edward T. Hall, in his 1976 book *Beyond Culture* coined as "low context" communication norms. Some patterns consistent with low context communication are the expectation that information be delivered in a linear and succinct fashion, that feedback is given directly and close to the event, and that "you say what you mean and you mean what you say." In other words, there are few embedded messages. I call this the Clint Eastwood approach to communication. Think about your college essays, the demand for one-page executive summaries, or the last presentation you gave. Linear. Succinct. PowerPoint. Three bullet points contained in one slide—ah, perfection!

Now, how do culture and communication fit together? I will use myself as an example. Though I am technically multi-racial, from a cultural point of view I identify as African American. Let me tell you about African Americans. We are expressive. Linear and succinct are a bit boring and unnatural for us. We are products of an African oral tradition and to this day we love flair. After all, we invented "the dozens," a spirited exchange of insults about family members, particularly mothers. And rap was born when urban East Coast youth drew upon Caribbean "toasting" and homegrown "boasting" traditions in folk poems to create a new art form that laid the path for great modern day storytellers and culture shapers like Jay Z. I can go on and on with examples from modern culture but am sure you understand the point; generally speaking, the Clint Eastwood approach is not what comes to mind when I reflect on my cultural heritage.

I have a vivid memory of being five or six years old and asking my father a very direct question; a "Why is the sky blue?" kind of question that is typical of kids that age. My father looked me dead in the eye and said, "Did I ever tell you the story about the hawk and the buzzard?" He continued with a straight, even serious, face after a long pause: "The hawk and the buzzard flew together for seven years and never exchanged a word between them. One day the hawk looks over to the buzzard and says, 'We've been flying kinda nice, haven't we?' The buzzard looks back and says, 'You know, you talk too damn much.'"

That was it. My Dad just stopped talking and walked away. What do you think, Reader? That about sums it up, right? How would your five- or six-year-old kid respond to that kind of answer? To this day when I get in one of my states and I'm going on about something, my Daddy just looks at me and says, "Did I ever tell you the story about the hawk and the buzzard?" That's high-context communication. There's a lot of meaning outside and coded within the nonverbal interaction. And this kind of communication, in the form of storytelling, is typical in high-context cultures.

Now imagine my difficulty getting through college, a setting where linear and succinct communication is the expectation. Though I am born and raised in the U.S. and English is my first language, I was in translation mode much of the time, constantly trying to figure out the rules for surviving in a low-context University environment without being adequately prepared. This, of course, was just the tip of the metaphoric iceberg. Moving from college into a professional environment only meant that the stakes got higher.

After 10+ years in the workforce, and just when I thought I had figured out how to ride the waves of culture within the U.S. context, I was asked to design and lead an "East/West-Leadership Institute and Cultural Exchange" between university administrators from some of the U.S.-based Ivy League universities and 30 of the most prominent universities in China. Chinese communication norms are much more high-context even than African American norms, and much, much more high-context than most U.S.-based universities. An example: from the moment we arrived in China until the moment we left, 10 days later, we were never without an escort. A Chinese ambassador was assigned to each of us and escorted us to every meal, meeting, and site-seeing opportunity. These ambassadors only left our sides at the end of each day after seeing to it that we were tucked away for the evening in our hotel rooms. Bright and early each morning our ambassadors were waiting at our hotel room doors to escort us to breakfast and through the next day's activities.

My Ivy League colleagues and the Clint Eastwood approach to communication would have been the norm on U.S. soil. Turning down a request to sing in front of strangers wouldn't be considered smug but "professional." But we were in China, where indirect, relationship-driven, nuance rich, exchanges were going to make or break the success of our event.

Karaoke began as the final courses of our meals were served and went well into the toasting rituals. Our Chinese counterparts would stand, one by one and sing full-length folk songs representing the regions from which they came. Some were from farming communities, others from fishing villages. The songs ranged from playful to beautifully expressive and pride-filled deliveries. To a person, everyone sang...except us.

One evening on a chartered bus to Beijing's famous Laoshe Tea House I huddled with my American colleagues—all of whom were sitting together on the front of the bus, sunk down in their seats to avoid the wireless microphone that was being passed around for karaoke. "Come on folks, we can do this," I said. "We are cultural ambassadors." And then I went on to remind them that we are coming from a low-context environment into a high-context one—very high context. In high-context communication, the relationship precedes the business. "If we aren't able to make genuine personal connections that allow us to form a trusting base, I'm afraid any of the other business goals we have in mind are destined to fail. We have to show our good will as human beings." Later that evening, after dinner and with a few more mini-pep talks, we did karaoke—as a group—but we did it. We stood, went to the front of the room and sang our great American folk round—"Row, Row, Row Your Boat." We were brilliant, and got a hearty standing ovation. With a huge smile of satisfaction on her face a dean from Princeton looked at me and said, "We should do one more." That was the tipping point in our trip. To this day those relationships continue to flourish.

The story is meant to illustrate the role identity plays in exploring your own multi-dimensionality, and underscore how culture works, and why it's so important to develop cultural dexterity. The norms that are going to help us manage relationships, manage global teams and negotiate business deals across cultures will be cultural norms. They may be difficult to know immediately at a deep level, but a robust understanding and skills set begins with self-knowledge and curiosity.

Bringing Together the Pieces

Who Are You?

Reflect:

Take time to reflect on the many dimensions of your identity and how they are interconnected. Consider your identity a complex and unique tapestry, with interconnecting aspects that allows your varied dimensions to be acknowledged and leveraged as part of your intentional leadership practice.

Irreplaceable

While you are thinking about all that you are and have to bring to your clients, colleagues and employers, also consider how they know you add value. My assertion here is that being authentic and multi-dimensional isn't enough. Someone else, and hopefully someone who matters, knows exactly what you bring and how it makes you indispensable—irreplaceable. Seth Godin, author and thought leader, describes irreplaceable people in organizations as "linchpins".

In my consulting work I meet an unfortunately low number of people who would describe themselves as linchpins. How do I know? I ask around. At the beginning of any consulting engagement I actively seek out people in the organization with ideas about how to "make things better around here." The big ideas about how to breathe new life into your organization shouldn't come from me, I'm a tourist. I care, but I'm going home, back to my office on Michigan Avenue at the end of the engagement. Linchpins are the people who have lived and will continue to live in the organization long after I leave. They have more skin in the game, and perspective, than I do (than does any consultant). So, I seek out these insightful people to help me get a sense of the client organization's capacity. Yep, linchpins often help me understand how much capacity—ability to grow—is possessed by an organization. And that, then, let's me know how hard to push, and in what direction.

Here's the other great thing about linchpins—they can be incredibly influential. They might not be influential when they first arrive in an organization or all the time, but they are the people who, armed with belief in their ideas and their organization's ability, build strategic alliances and create breakthrough experiences. They stick their necks out when others are in protecting their necks mode, like turtles tucked safely inside their shells. Don't get me wrong, I'm not encouraging you to go into your next meeting like a bull in a China shop, pushing an idea that's been percolating in your head for weeks but has never been vetted. Influence is more than just having a great idea—it's about understanding and being able to carefully navigate the environment and relationships needed to get the idea socialized, perhaps massaged a bit and considered viable by others.

Alas, I think there's more linchpin potential but so many of the people I meet in organizations are paralyzed by fear, waiting for the "person in charge" to give direction, even when the person in charge is paralyzed by fear himself. The leadership challenge is being able to get beyond fear of exposure or perceived weakness in times when others are in need of a new approach. Indispensable people are able to let go, at least temporarily, of the need for approval. Assume that coloring in the lines is for the boring and the brainwashed. Let go of the little voice in your head that so desperately wants an "A". Know that you have inside the ability, and the courage, to create something—a relationship, a culture within your unit, a new product or system or offering—that others may not immediately approve of nor understand, but that adds value.

Take-Aways for Making Yourself Irreplaceable:

1. **Believe you are irreplaceable.** *This is HUGE. If you don't see your contribution, or potential contribution, as unique, how will others?*

2. **Pull your head up, away from the fires and the tedious tasks, and look around.** *So many people are drowning in the time- and energy-consuming operational realities of life which squeeze out time from the strategic endeavors. The difference between everyone else and leaders is this, leaders are strategic. Leaders find opportunities to effect systems, not just cross off the ever-replenishing "to do" list items.*

3. **Find, acknowledge, embrace and cultivate your creativity.** *Many of us spend much of the day using the left sides of our brains—the analytical, objective, "there is ONE right answer" side. Find ways to tap into the right side of your brain more regularly—the intuitive, thoughtful and subjective side. Take an art class, or take a walk through an art gallery during your lunch break. We may want to take objective approaches to leading, but in reality, we live In subjective organizations where being able to read subtle cues, use intuition, and thoughtfully navigate your own emotion and those of others (e.g. emotional intelligence) are invaluable characteristics.*

4. **Access your whole self.** *We are more than just heads sitting propped up on hunched shoulders slouching over computers. Stand up. Take a walk. Stop thinking about work—several times per day. Incorporate walking meditation into each day: letting yourself be overwhelmed by the beauty of the trees changing color or feel the crisp morning air on your face while freeing your mind of negative thoughts. Then go back to your workplace feeling refreshed and open to new ideas for solving the problems that will inevitably still be just where you left them.*

5. **Help others.** *Recently, I posed this question to a panel of executives, "What are the top qualities you look for in future leaders?" Their responses included, "willingness to step forward," "helpfulness," and "can do attitude." Show yourself to be a team player and willing to step up and take on opportunities to be helpful to others without being asked or in need of reward.*
   Helping others allows you to:
   - deepen your skill set (teaching someone is a wonderful way to learn),
   - cultivate genuine (and strategic) relationships with colleagues and potential colleagues,
   - gather additional insight about a system that may need to be changed, and
   - demonstrate your expertise.

Strategy 2:
Create a Clear, Compelling and Shared Vision

Have you ever felt like you have drifted into certain experiences? What about your career? Or drifted into a leadership role? If you said yes, you are not alone. Many people drift into opportunity and then figure out how to "skill up" to meet the new demands. Life happens and despite even the most diligent planning efforts, serendipity has a way of popping on the scenes of our lives when we least expect it.

On the other hand, long-term drifting doesn't position you with the greatest amount of agency possible in your journey. Drifting often takes the form of making choices based on what a person doesn't want—in a job, in pay, in a boss. Putting yourself in reaction mode means that you will, over time, take as many steps backward as forward. You will need to constantly reposition, hoping to find a more comfortable existence. After years of effort, you will likely have a built-up lack of fulfillment—a wanting more.

This "wanting more" state is painful. It's like death by a thousand cuts. It is also a very popular state of existence for a lot of people, and women in particular. We settle. We have a little whisper in our ear —coming from our gut or the Universe— that gets ignored, even suppressed.

We experience slight insults—nibbles—at work about our communication style, our style of dress, our credentials. We experience little nibbles from our friends—subtle comments about our weight, our career stall, our choice in a partner. We experience little nibbles from family members—guilt-laden messages about our priorities. Yet day-in and day-out we continue to invest in these relationships and hold our tongue.

We look around at our friends, sisters, colleagues and rationalize, "My life is like so many other people's." Or "The guilt I'm feeling is just a woman's burden to bear." We give ourselves mental pep talks about being thankful for the good things and remembering those who have it far worse. We are accustomed to feeling moderately overworked and underappreciated. We acknowledge that we're living in a man's world, *the man's* world. All the while we want more, you want more. You know you have more inside of you than you have accessed thus far. You know it's time for a change.

All change starts with a vision. A vision is a vivid and compelling end state—an aspired-for destination. Vivid means that you should be able to close your eyes and see the vision in detail, including seeing yourself in it. A compelling vision is one that is so enticing that you cannot help but act in a way that brings it into being. It is powerful enough to stimulate energy that makes you literally jump out of bed in the morning, or stay up all night, or do whatever it takes to make it become reality.

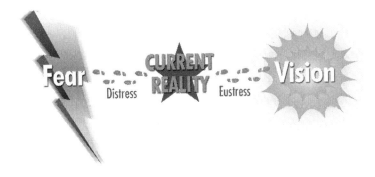

The Power of Vision

In the absence of a compelling vision people tend to focus primarily on fear—the "what if's" associated with not having a clear sense of the future. The energy used is called distress, or negative emotional stress. Stressful energy is what we use to worry. We worry about paying our bills, worry about our kids' behavior, worry about the tension-filled relationship with our colleague, worry about holding on to the client on whom our business depends. As you know, this kind of energy is emotionally exhausting.

The human brain is wired so that when we feel fear manifested in forms such as stress, worry, threat or embarrassment, a part of the brain called the amygdala triggers a cortisol release into our bloodstream. The cortisol then redirects resources from the analytical, problem-solving, thinking part of the brain to the extremities—our arms and hands, legs and feet. It puts us into the primal "fight, flight or flee" mode, which is the survival-oriented wiring humans have had for thousands of years. Fight, flight or flee were viable options when humans were running from bears or warring clans, but it's much less appropriate in modern times when running from a stressful or embarrassing situation is typically the least useful response. Nowadays, having access to the analytical, problem-solving, thinking part of our brain, particularly in fear-filled situations, would be much more helpful.

Think of the last time you had a disagreement with your boss, or colleague, or spouse. Do you remember how you felt? If you had an argument, think of what you said at the time, then what you wish you had said after having some time to reflect on the exchange. Isn't that how it goes—two days later you're standing in the shower and exactly the right words come to your mind? That's because the immediate threat has been removed. Your emotional state then levels out and the fullest resources go back to feeding the rational, creative, problem-solving part of your brain. It is important to understand this cortisol release in response to input that elicits fear because we are bombarded daily by stimuli that can trigger our amygdala.

Think back again to the argument you had in your mind a few sentences ago. What happened directly after that argument? What did you do next? Did you have another unpleasant experience? It's likely you did. Do you know why? Because the cortisol that was released in your body from the first argument takes two to three hours to wear off. In the meantime, your amygdala is a hair trigger. The next minor infraction is just adding the proverbial fuel to the fire emotionally speaking. It's why you go from having a bad experience to having a bad day. Familiar? It explains a lot, doesn't it?

It's important to remember that humans are wired to have emotional responses. Emotion is not a bad thing, it just is. In fact, we have emotional responses to stimuli before we have rational ones. This is why marketing specialists focus on which colors or scents elicit an increased propensity for buying and what kind of background music playing in a store is most likely to lessen the inhibition to spend money. Emotions are powerful—in either direction. Emotions that focus on fear are powerfully able to cause distress. Emotions that focus on vision are powerfully able to stimulate eustress—creativity, the energy needed to bring something new into being.

So there is hope for better management of our energy, and the energy of our employees, colleagues and clients. We can shift our focus to vision.
Close your eyes and think about something you have created in the past. It can

be anything at all—a database, a cake from scratch, a website, a business, a child. Now remember the process of bringing that new thing into being. Was it challenging? Painful at times? Did you stretch beyond your comfort zone? Were you in constant learner mode?

Now think about the outcome of your efforts? When you look at your creation, how do you feel? How do others feel about it? How do others feel about you after witnessing the effort and the outcome? My expectation is that those of you who actually thought about a personal creation and the outcomes associated with it are feeling a bit of a tingle right now.

The emotions you are feeling are so powerful that they can be activated by merely remembering something we did that made us proud. I think about my son. Whew, that was some work! Sure, I recall sleepless nights that were my constant reality during his first two years. I think about the temper tantrums and emergency room visits. But those memories are far from prevalent in my mind. Every day I look into his face with the greatest feeling of satisfaction and love possible. I have grown as a person, feeling the fullest range of human emotions—fear, anxiety, impatience, gratitude, pride, extraordinary love—because I had a vision of being a great mother. That vision is still so compelling that I jump out of bed every day and do anything necessary to contribute to its sustenance. That's eustress—the energy used to fuel pursuit of a vision.

Eustress is the kind of stress that produces positive feelings and a sense of fulfillment. The feeling is not associated with the stressor itself, rather how the stressor is perceived, which changes depending on positive feelings such as control or healthy challenge. Eustress allows us to feel satisfaction, hope or meaning as a result of our effort.

Once you have identified a vivid and compelling vision for yourself then you can use the positive energy produced through pursuit of that vision to fuel your continued effort. Now think about your current reality. What does your life look like right now? Is it calling for a massive overhaul? Is it mostly good but could use some strategic choices and actions to get you out of drift mode and onto the path of your vision?

Listen. If you need to make a significant change, please don't just make a mental acknowledgement. Say it out loud. Don't just say what's not working. Use this as the moment to shift from the negative to the affirmative, from focusing on fear to focusing on aspiration.

What do you want? Close your eyes. Do you see it? Is it so compelling that it will catapult you out of bed tomorrow morning? If not, you still have some work to do. If so, get going. Start telling people, anyone who will listen, about your vision.

Of course there will be naysayers. Ignore them. Listen to their dissenting points of view so that any insight that might be present in their comments is considered on your journey, but do not let them slow you down. Heck, let the naysayers speed up your progress; give you a bit of ammunition. Let this be your moment to show 'em what you got!

This next step may be a huge risk for you, or feel like one, at least. You probably have a life that is "just fine". You likely have a relatively stable job or career, a small but steady stream of clients, a personal life that isn't glamorous but not laughable, either. Not rocking the boat has worked for you. You have avoided great reward, but you've also, and perhaps smartly, mitigated risk. On the other hand, do you find yourself swallowing your pride by taking on tasks that were menial compared to your actual skill set; not raising prices because you're afraid to lose that long-time client? Are you avoiding re-branding and branching out because you are concerned that your worthiness may not be immediately recognized by the market?

I did this for almost two decades because in my head I kept telling myself that I should feel thankful for what I have; that especially in this economy, I need to realize that others have it much worse. Most of all, I accepted that reality because I didn't have a vision for what I truly wanted for myself. I just knew what I didn't want – to be vulnerable when I was used to be an expert. I didn't want to lose all that I had spent so many years to build. I didn't want to be a failure and broke.

I was focused on fear, not vision. Focusing on vision would have forced to think concretely about aspiration. Focusing on aspiration means that attention and intention is on what one wants to become. Perhaps you want to build a blog that earns enough revenue to pay your full-time salary. Or you want to build a business that is robust enough to be purchased. Or you want to create something new and innovative? Any of these visions requires measured risk, and a willingness to be vulnerable. Further, attaining any of these visions requires the opposite of drift—they require intentionality.

Make sure your vision is crisp. It should speak to you. You may hear criticisms. Listen to them and allow yourself to be open to making needed adjustments without letting go of the core. Your vision has to be something about which you are passionate, not a watered down compromise that's more focused on mitigating risk than making an impact. Remember, it's your vision and it may take a bit of time for others to come around.

First Assess Your Current Reality

In preparing to create your vision, begin with an honest assessment of where things are today – your current reality. All of us have a sense of what's going on inside and around us: from what's keeping you at a job you're not crazy about to the triggers that lead to late night refrigerator raids. Many of us do not, however, think about those things systematically; that is, within the same context.

Further, we may not think about them often enough. Perhaps you think about the area of your life that is giving you the most discomfort at a particular point in time. You then turn more attention to complaining about and/or fixing that part of your life. Once the issue has resolved itself (which never happens) or you have fixed it, your attention shifts to another area of your life that demands immediate attention. You are careful not to look back to the previous area for fear that some untended remnant of the previously dealt with problem will reappear.

A periodic and more holistic analysis of your life's landscape is a more effective approach. You experience changes in your life regularly: new job, new title, new job responsibilities without a new title, new apartment, new client, new idea. Things change. It's important to look at your life's situation regularly because the changes often occur without pausing to understand their implications, as well as potential opportunities afforded by these changes. The worksheet on the following page will allow you to begin looking inside and around you, and then make some notes about the current reality of your life. Avoid listing overly broad answers—drill down as much as possible so that the answers are meaningful for you, and specific enough to allow you to refer to them as you begin constructing your vision.

Assessing Your Current Reality Worksheet

Questions	Answers
What three areas of your life currently demand most of your time?	
What informs these priorities?	
What life changes did you make in the past 12-18 months to respond to changing to these priorities?	
What changes are you planning to make within the next 12-18 months? Why these? How are you deciding upon these?	
What are some of the factors outside your control that will influence your ability to make the above-mentioned choices?	

After completing the Assessing Your Current Reality Worksheet look back over your answers. Reflect on what you wrote. Are your answers specific? Are they addressing the most important parts of your current reality? Are your answers honest? Let me restate—an honest description of your current reality is needed. It's impossible to create an accurate roadmap to your vision unless you can identify a beginning point.

Once you are comfortable with your understanding of current reality—pause. How do you feel when you think about it? A bit frustrated? Anxious? Anticipatory? Great! Now point yourself forward, not back, and let the eustress kick in!

Strategy 3:
Take Control of Your Brand

Getting Started Exercise

When you hear the word "leader" who immediately comes to mind? You're not alone if Gandhi, Dr. Martin Luther King, Jr., Mother Theresa or some other "bigger than life" person came to mind. It has been my experience that most people think of leaders as someone other than themselves. When asked to reflect on why this might be the case, even considering their formal and informal roles and spans of influence, people typically say what might be described as leading feels like "just doing my job" when applied to themselves. It may seem that this approach is humble and doesn't pose a problem. But actually not seeing oneself as a leader means that the definition of a leader is being applied with too narrow a brush stroke and the opportunity for understanding leadership traits from a developmental point of view is lost.

If I believed that all great leaders were born to be such I would not have bothered writing this book. There would be no need investing in understanding which characteristics are possessed and behaviors practiced by effective leaders if only to satisfy an intellectual curiosity. On the contrary, I firmly believe that leadership is more about traits that are developed by deliberate choice and effort. This isn't to say that effort typically begins with an aspiration to be a leader, per se. Instead, choice and effort are typically driven by a desire to accomplish something great, without conscious regard for accolades. Dr. King, Mother Theresa, and Mahatma Gandhi were also doing their jobs. Their choices were driven by a passion and conviction to create social and cultural changes, not with the goal in mind to be internationally recognized leaders. Yet through the choices each made, their goals were accomplished and they had a huge impact on the world.

My approach to brand management builds on research, takes into consideration your unique attributes and assets, and encourages you to set a benchmark that truly resonates with you—the person you want to be known as rather than a prescription that worked for someone else. My approach connects brand with the ability to be influential, to leverage the name and reputation you have built and will continue to build up. It includes reflecting and then linking your intentional practice to three essential arenas:

1. Identifying what you want through clear articulation of your vision, passion and strengths;

2. Understanding what you can leverage, through your unique voice and the context (multi-dimensionality); and

3. Positioning yourself for leverage, through accessing the value of your personal brand.

Brand Development Essentials

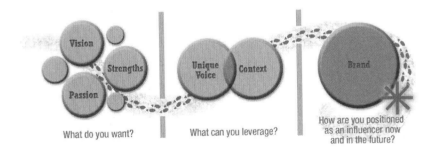

What do you want?   What can you leverage?   How are you positioned as an influencer now and in the future?

Building Your Brand

There have been countless studies conducted over time and in various contexts, leading to a plethora of leadership characteristics. There are as many different ranking systems for leadership characteristics as lists themselves. One of my personal favorites, though, is an approach used by David Campbell, whose groundbreaking work on career development made him renowned in the field of industrial and organizational psychology. Campbell created the "Campbell Leadership Descriptor" designed specifically for use in situations where comprehensive analysis of leadership characteristics is useful.

The Campbell Leadership Descriptor draws on years of research conducted on senior level leaders, representing mostly corporate entities but spanning a variety of countries and national cultures, who participated in developmental experiences as well as studies of prominent leaders from previous periods of history. The Descriptor forces an association of leadership with people within reach—and then a self-application. This allows leadership to be understood in its component parts rather than as one big, amorphous gift given to only a chosen few.

Building on the intention of Campbell's instrument, I've created a Personal Brand Comparison Exercise as a technique for benchmarking your brand against a person who you consider to have a positive brand and a person you consider to have a negative or lacking brand.

Personal Brand Comparison Exercise

<u>WELL-BRANDED PERSON</u>

Step 1: Think about a person, whom you know, who has a powerful and positive personal brand.

Insert name here:

Step 2: Now think about what makes that person's brand so attractive to you and others.

- What kind of energy does the person project?

- About what does the person talk?

- What kind of language does she/he use?

- What would you describe as his/her passions? Aspirations? Values? Vision?

- What kinds of habits are included in this person's routine?

- With whom does he/she associate?

- How does this person exert influence? Describe the specific tactics or strategies that you've seen employed.

- How does she/he dress? Eat? Relax? Play? Learn? Work? Travel?

- When others talk about her/him, what do they say?

POORLY-BRANDED PERSON

Step 3: Think about a person, whom you know, who has a negative or lacking personal brand.

Insert name here:

Step 4: Now think about what makes that person's brand so unattractive to you and others.

- What kind of energy does the person project?

- About what does the person talk?

- What kind of language does she/he use?

- What would you describe as his/her passions? Aspirations? Values? Vision?

- What kinds of habits are included in this person's routine?

- With whom does he/she associate?

- How does this person exert influence? Describe the specific tactics or strategies that you've seen employed.

- How does she/he dress? Eat? Relax? Play? Learn? Work? Travel?

- When others talk about her/him, what do they say?

<u>YOU</u>

Step 5: Now think about yourself.

- What kind of energy do you project?

- About what do you talk?

- What kind of language do you use?

- What would others, with whom you have regular association, describe as your passions? Aspirations? Values? Vision?

- What kinds of habits are included in your daily/weekly routine?

- With whom do you associate? Are they your aspirational peer group? Are they doing as well as you are personally and professionally? When others see you together, do your associates reflect well on you?

- How do you exert influence? Describe the specific tactics or strategies that you regularly employ?

- How do you dress? Eat? Relax? Play? Learn? Work? Travel?

- When you're not around, what do others say about you?

Step 6: After you have completed the exercise, compare the answers. Where is there good overlap? And where are the gaps? What can you do to close the gaps—between where you are now and characteristics possessed by your well-branded leader?

When you consider your brand, think honestly about what others see. People only know what you tell them. The rest of what is assumed about you is just that – an assumption often based on speculation or guessing. Think about what you want to convey to other people, even without having to say it directly.

Brand links closely with identity. You have a large say over it, but other people's perception counts. A great example of a person who manages her brand with intention is Olympic Gold Medalist April Holmes. April is touted as the world's fastest female amputee. She has shared stories with me about companies, before agreeing to sponsor her, that have reviewed every tweet that had ever come from her Twitter account, read every article that had ever been written about her, and watched every interview she had ever given. Representatives from these companies compliment her about her public presentation—everything was not only squeaky clean, but it was filled with positive messages of encouragement to fellow athletes, praise for her sponsors, and overall classiness. Your brand is what you portray about yourself all the time, everywhere, and can translate into business deals (or not) worth big bucks.

A couple of things to remember about managing your brand:

1. Let go of the guilt. Not being "on" 100% of the time is okay. Sometimes people won't perceive you the way you want to be perceived. But give it your best shot anyway and know that your effort was honorable.

2. Don't be a jerk. Treat people well.

3. Don't gossip and avoid the company of gossips. It's unattractive in any light.

4. Share personal information in moderation. Know that some people will always find fault in you. Don't help them.

5. Stand for something but don't be inflexible. The moment you stop listening is the moment you lose some ability to influence.

6. Don't worry about what other people say. Be authentic and true to yourself. Know when to keep doors open, and know when to close them.

7. Stay above the fray. When you have the choice, always chose the high road.

8. Be credible. Do what you say you will do.

9. Beware of overusing your strengths (e.g. charm). In high doses, they can become flaws.

10. Choose happiness. Begin acting in accordance immediately.

Reflection:

For what are you known?
If a stranger looked at you, your website, your social media activity, the quality of the products or services you offer, what impression would she have about you? What do your colleagues and clients say about you when you're not around?

Leadership Take-Away:

Make a list of five behavioral shifts you make in order to have a positive impact on your brand.

1. I will...

2. I will...

3. I will...

4. I will...

5. I will...

Strategy 4:
Think Wholly and Unplug

One of the most common stem sentences I hear from executives and mid-level managers alike is, "Give me the 3 steps to...." Sometimes the end of the sentence is "...motivate my staff" or "be more influential" but the desire for sound bites is a constant. Why? My clients are like many of us, practical, results-oriented (e.g. looking for immediate answers) and living in a world filled with information but not enough time to take it all in, never mind figuring what to do with it.

Though I understand the pressure-filled world within which so many of us live and are expected to perform, it's difficult to imagine truly impactful leaders blossoming out of chaos and armed only with sound bites of wisdom. Deep, meaningful, nuanced practice is informed by discipline over time. There are no short cuts to wisdom. Further, wise people intentionally and consistently tend to the whole self.

The logical place to begin is with the mind, right? I don't know if I should admit this here, but I often struggle to think clearly. There are plenty of times when I can't remember what city I was in the previous week. I feel like the barrage of emails, texts and alerts that I'm expected to compute minute-by-minute is making it difficult for me to think.

I'm not alone. Scientific studies have shown that although interaction with technology can have a beneficial effect—faster reaction time and sharpened logical thinking—overall it's making us less intelligent, less engaged and is battering our memories. "The human brain is under threat from the modern world," says neuroscientist Baroness Susan Greenfield, professor of pharmacology at Oxford University. "Electronic devices have an impact on the microcellular structure and biochemistry of our brains."

The demands of work and other recent social constructs have led scientists to coin the neurological phenomenon "popcorn brain"— switching quickly between tasks and digesting small bits of surface-level information to keep our minds constantly stimulated. Further, when we do sit down to work, the constant interruptions mean our productivity levels are low. Studies have found that the average worker gets only 11 minutes between each interruption, and it takes an average of 25 minutes to return fully to the task at hand. Further, "heavy technology users are likely to develop the left side of their brains, leaving the right side untapped," says Dr. Byun Gi-Won of the Balance Brain Centre in Seoul. The right side is linked with concentration, so our attention and memory span are therefore reduced. The left side has its uses—it's in charge of language, logic and mathematical computations—the reason why people who play more video games are often good at solving problems, and why heavy tech users might experience an increase in the brain's reaction time—thinking quicker but not as clearly.

Recent studies have shown that, on average, we are exposed 8.5 hours a day to digital technology; enough to over time change the brain's structure. According to Dr. Greenfield, "the brain is not the unchanging organ that we might imagine. It is shaped by what we do to it and the experience of daily life." This rewiring of our brain as a result of everyday experiences is called neuroplasticity. In the worst cases, our intricate neural pathways are being destroyed because certain synaptic connections (such as those that occur when we think deeply) become neglected and weaken if we favor quicker ways of receiving information (such as short news items). The bigger picture effect is that we are less able to process and remember information over time. In a study published in 2011, researchers in China gave MRI scans to 18 students who spent about 10 hours a day online. They found that some students had decreased grey matter volume in the bilateral dorsolateral prefrontal cortex (the thinking part of the brain), which would, in extreme cases lead to lower cognitive function. This part of the brain is also responsible for motor skills, working memory and our general intellect.

Also, because our brains are constantly being stimulated with information, we are not giving enough downtime to formulate new memories. Scientists at the University of California discovered that when rats have a new experience, such as exploring an unfamiliar area, their brains show new patterns of activity. It's only when the rats take a break from their exploration that they process those patterns in a way that seems to create a lasting memory of those experiences. Simply put, the rats internalize the learning only if the new experience is followed by a break. In yoga, this break is called shavasana.

The word shavasana comes from the Sanskrit words Sava meaning "corpse", and Asana meaning "posture" or "seat". Literally, shavasana is known as corpse pose. Yogis say that shavasana is the most important of yoga postures, allowing the body, mind, and spirit to be rejuvenated.

This is what Wikipedia has to say about the posture's benefits.

> *"After the exertions of the practice, shavasana allows the body a chance to regroup and reset itself. After a balanced practice, the entire body will have been stretched, contracted, twisted and inverted. This means that even the deepest muscles will have the opportunity to let go and shed their regular habits, if only for a few minutes.*
>
> *Furthermore, the physiological benefits of deep relaxation are numerous and include:*

- a decrease in heart rate and the rate of respiration,
- a decrease in blood pressure,
- a decrease in muscle tension,
- a decrease in metabolic rate and the consumption of oxygen,
- a reduction in general anxiety,
- a reduction in the number and frequency of anxiety attacks,
- an increase in energy levels and in general productivity,
- an improvement in concentration and in memory,
- an increase in focus,
- a decrease in fatigue, coupled with deeper and sounder sleep, and improved self-confidence.

Yogi or not, the above list of benefits will enhance any developmental journey. Your own spilling over plate will most likely continue to be piled onto. Your ability to manage, with skill and grace, the demands depends on the level and quality of your personal resources. You are not a robot. You have finite resources and replenishing them requires a disciplined investment—and investment that no one will make for you. If you won't unplug as a gift to yourself, unplug because the cost of continuing to move at break-neck pace is too high.

A Holistic Approach

The transition made in this section, from mind to body and now back to mind again, is consistent with contemporary leadership development doctrine. It is commonplace to see dozens of books on psychology and neuroscience lining the business section shelves in libraries and popular bookstores. Thankfully, our modern understanding of personal and business best practice has been heavily influenced by the combination of Western culture's desire for a logical—even skeptical—approach to discovery with Eastern philosophies that build on thousand year old truths and practices; often incorporating spiritual and emotional aspects of human realities. At this stage in our understanding, we are replete with scientific evidence that underscores the importance of tapping into both the left and right sides of our brain's functions, and tending our intellectual, emotional, physical and spiritual (or meaning-seeking) selves.

<u>Leadership Take-Away:</u>

Make notes about how you will incorporate more shavasana into your life.

Here are a few examples of ways that you might build more replenishing time into your life.

1. Practice yoga regularly.

2. Meditate. Take a class, spend dedicated time every morning or evening, or even insert small amounts of time into your day, at your desk, or in between meetings.

3. Take a walk during lunch or try one of Steve Job's famous "walking meetings". Pay attention to the nature around you rather than using that time to check FB or worry about the pile of work waiting at your desk.

4. Journal. Create a reflection journal and make notes to yourself every day, emphasizing the day's observations of beauty or kindness. Describe experiences that made you feel good and you can extend on them.

5. Slow down. Be present. Pay attention to where you are now and the people who are with you.

Strategy 5:
Set a Positive Tone

Y ou have a higher probability of reaching maximum effectiveness if you begin with an assumption of abundance (of resources and options) rather than scarcity. This ability to anchor to positives is a profound asset, and has been proven to yield significant returns. Positive affect has been shown to lead to greater creativity, flexible thinking, as well as increased negotiation and problem-solving skills. People experiencing positive versus negative affect were found to be more ingenious and innovative when solving problems. Research measuring positive affect among medical personnel show that those students high in positive affect were more efficient, less confused, and more thorough in patient diagnosis than other medical students. Isn't this what we want for ourselves all the time—the ability to be high-functioning and happy?

The tricky thing about positive development is that understanding it isn't enough simply to reap its rewards. We have to internalize it into our belief system then behave in a manner consistent with those beliefs. We have to model these behaviors as part of our regular routine, with everyone we interact with, and even under pressure. It has to become part of the fabric of who are as human beings.

As a backdrop for discussing behavioral change, let's begin with a research-based understanding of positivity, drawn heavily from the work of Barbara Frederickson. In her 2009 book, Positivity, Frederickson outlines key concepts, definitions and benefits that are useful to share here.

1. Positivity is the key ingredient for flourishing. Its absence can lead to languishing. Flourishing and languishing aren't just Frederickson's gut assumptions. There are years and years' worth of scientific data, collected separately by different researchers and using various methods, that have arrived at the same conclusion. It's also been proven that flourishing and languishing associated with one's propensity for positive versus negative emotions applies to individuals and groups, such as work teams.

2. Positivity is different, and more specific, than happiness. The emotions included in the positivity spectrum include:

Joy *Gratitude*

Serenity

Interest Hope

Pride Amusement

INSPIRATION

Awe *Love*

Each of the above emotions should be explored and experienced with as much regularity as possible, which creates upward spiral trends in our emotions. The goal is a 3:1 ratio, positive to negative emotions.

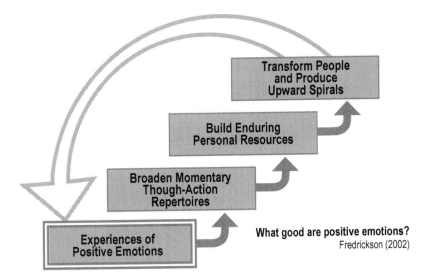

What good are positive emotions?
Fredrickson (2002)

3. As early as 2002, Frederickson began publishing responses to the research question "What good are positive emotions?" She found then, and has continuously built research-based evidence for the theory she coined "Broaden and Build." In essence, positivity has been scientifically

proven to **a)** *broaden*—open up our thinking about an experience, and **b)** *build*, create a foundation upon which new ideas and relationships can be born. Further, people with high positivity ratios are found to be more *resilient* during tough times.

It is possible to increase your positivity ratio and create upward spirals in your own life and that allow you to flourish—have breakthrough experiences that otherwise would have not been available. Techniques for increasing your positivity ratio include:

- Be more aware of the various positive emotions and consciously tapping into them as much as possible—especially love.

- Learn to meditate, practice yoga or keep a reflection journal.

- Slow down, shift your environment, get in touch with nature (being outside, especially during good weather, has been found to have a positive effect on human's emotions).

- Surround yourself with people you love as often as possible.

- Focus externally—happiness cannot be directly pursued, it must ensue as an outcome of a meaning-filled life. Focus on others and the good you can bring them, with a genuinely open heart, and you will flourish.

As leaders, also think about how you establish and nurture a positive tone for your team. You don't have to be a naturally "upbeat" person to foster a positive environment within which your team can flourish. Think about some of these options:

- Capitalize on positive events daily.

- Work toward a positive to negative interaction ratio of 6:1. Teams that use constructive language more often are found to be more productive and innovative.

- Give feedback that acknowledges the role of positive emotions in daily work. In other words, tell people how their positive behaviors are having a desirable impact on you, your clients, and their work.

- Lead in a manner that is consistent with your values. Model positive behaviors including self-efficacy, hope, optimism, moral efficacy, resilience. Ask for feedback on the extent to which your behavior is consistent with your values and the quality of your modeling behavior.

A final point about positivity: practice it now. Don't wait until times get tough to try to recall some bullet point wisdom for managing through crisis. In times of crisis, people resort to doing whatever it is that they have practiced most up to that point. So if you've been treating people badly until now, when times are tough you will probably continue to do just that. And it won't help you, or them.

Instead, think deliberately—now—about how you want to be perceived and the impact you want to have on people. Begin putting into practice actions that will help you make strides in that direction. Then, when times do get tough – and they will – your amygdala is less apt to be hijacked by fear because you have embedded thoughtful responses into your repertoire. You will be able to access more easily the helpful behaviors when you need them, rather than stuck in fight, flight or freeze mode.

Further, because you have been practicing behaviors that are positively impacting others and managing their perception of you, you will have built rapport for yourself. Even if you make a mistake here and there, the good rapport that you have built might buy you a "pass." I like to say, "We judge others based on their behaviors but we judge ourselves based on our intentions." Making your good intentions known early on and often allow others to be less critical, as we are with ourselves, in times of crisis or when mistakes are made.

BEHAVIOR/IMPACT ANALYSIS

The **Behavior/Impact Analysis** is a practical tool for reflecting on your behavior and its impact. This is a tool that you can use on your own or with a mentor. It can be applied to behaviors in any context—work, school, or interpersonal relationships.

Exercise: *Reflect on a particular behavior that you exhibited. Describe it in the left column. Do not attribute motives or intentions here. Try to just describe the behavior as another person would see and judge it. After you have made some notes about the behavior, describe the implications of the behavior in the next three columns.*

My behavior	My behavior's impact on the relationship	My behavior's impact on how I am perceived by others	My behavior's implication on my vision

It is important to understand the benefits and costs, to your personal brand, of certain behaviors. Once you have completed the reflective exercise, think about steps that you should take to either a) repeat or extend a behavior that you believe is having a positive effect on your brand or b) change or recover from a behavior that you believe is having a negative effect on your brand. I also encourage you to go one step further—to seek out additional input on reflections. This could come from a mentor or a friend, or even better, from the person or group who was involved in the initial behavior described in the left column.

Strategy 6:
Ooze Passion

I am passionate about my work. I am passionate about discovery--discovering solutions for my clients and discovering hidden potential within myself. And that passion fuels the dogged pursuit of my vision. You may be thinking, "dogged pursuit of vision sounds nice but what does that mean in real-people words and given the complicated lives that real people live? Where does the energy come from?" Here's my answer: Aspiration must be fueled by a kind of personal zeal for achievement of specific goals. Aspiration must be fueled by passion.

A 2010 blog post by Rosabeth Moss Kanter, entitled "Does Your Passion Match Your Aspiration?" hits the nail on the head. Those of you familiar with Kanter's work know that she's a guru in the fields of leadership, change management and organizational development. In her post she says, "Leaders who create extraordinary new possibilities are passionate about their mission and are tenacious in pursuit of it. Many people have good ideas, but many fewer are willing to put themselves on the line for them. Passion separates good intentions and opportunism from real accomplishments."

This sort of passion is what I think we mean when we talk about "accountability", "customer service" and "engagement." The explicit acknowledgment of passion in pursuit of our mission and vision is more powerful because it wells from an internal source of motivation, the key to securing commitment.

Reflection:

1. Think about what fuels your passion at a personal level—and what you do to regularly re-fuel it. For me, I have a super-cool, five-year old son, Shiloh, aka PIP (Passion-in-a-Person). His well-spring of passion for everything is a beautiful reminder for me to stay connected to my own inner sense of curiosity and wonder.

2. As a leader, how might you more explicitly integrate the expectation of passion (as in "passionate pursuit of excellence" or "passionate about delivering the highest quality customer experience") into your organization's language and behavioral norms? How can passion inform your performance planning discussions, strategic planning or other organizational change processes?

Strategy 7:
Play to Your Strengths and Theirs

People have varied interests and experiences that shape their paths. Identifying and then leveraging your strengths is a key component in developing yourself. How do you know your strengths? Here's the formula:

Natural Talent

+

Enough Interest to Commit to Ongoing Practice

=

STRENGTH

Most of us are born with some natural talent, whether or not we have fully maximized it is another story. For now, think about the things that you are naturally good at: Are you athletic? Are you good with math? Are you a strong writer? Are you a good listener?

Next, what do you enjoy doing enough that you are willing to spend time investing in getting better at it? What is it that you do for sheer enjoyment with no regard for income-earning potential? Your strength can be found where the talent and the interest intersect. On the other hand, interests may be just that and nothing more. Know the difference.

I am 5'6" and camera shy. Sometimes I wonder if I am camera shy because I'm never satisfied with pictures of myself or the other way around. Either way, I've never been willing to spend too much time in front of a camera because it's agonizingly painful for me to try to figure out how to pose. Do I smile or not smile? What do I do with my hands? Is the person with the camera ever going to take the darn shot? And my bottom line is that I know I am going to be disappointed with the photo anyway.

When I was about 15 years old I was scouted to model. Of course I was thrilled and flattered, and enthusiastically started taking classes and putting together a portfolio. I loved runway work and went on to do a few local shows—every time with me as a major contributor. At some point, though, one of my instructors sat me down for a heart-to-heart.

"You're pretty, but in a cute girl-next-door sort of way. Your features aren't unique, pronounced or distinctive. On top of that, you're too short to go any farther with runway. It's time you turn your energy to print and television."

Imagine my disappointment. The only option I had for pursuing my then dream was to focus solely on work that required me to be in front of the dreaded cameras. That was it; my modeling aspirations ended that day. I didn't have the innate qualities for runway nor the interest (and confidence) to potentially increase my camera presence. I just didn't have what it took to turn modeling from an interest into a personal strength.

What are the take-aways from this story? Well, for me, I could have sought another opinion. The person who advised me was one person with one opinion. If my interest had been stronger, I probably would have consulted with more people about my chances as a model. Other opinions or a strong champion may have led me to invest the time and energy needed to become more comfortable in front of a camera.

Lessons:

- Don't sell yourself short.

- Before you go self-assessing your strengths and making life-altering decisions based on your own skewed self-image, get feedback.

- Sometimes an interest really is not and will not ever become a personal strength—maybe a hobby, but not necessarily a personal strength. Know when that's the case, too.

I advise you to use structured methods for gathering and analyzing data. It may seem overly formal, but structure builds discipline into your practice and allows you to create a benchmark against which you can track progress over time. Even a simple structured process could be helpful to gain insight about your preferences and potential areas of strength. Try tools like self-evaluations, which can be formal or informal. For example, an informal evaluation could be as simple as a journaling exercise where you answer the following five questions:

1. If I could choose any career and money were not a factor, what would it be? Why?

2. I am regularly praised when I _____?

3. If I had to write a personal essay in five words, what words would best capture my essence?

4. If I could take a 6-week course on any subject, I would choose _____.

5. I feel most proud of myself when I _____.

After you have answered these questions for yourself, invite a trusted friend or mentor to have a discussion with you. Share the questions in advance and ask her to come to your meeting prepared to share her answers. Discuss the similarities and differences in your answers. What conclusions can you now draw about your strengths? Are there any areas or answers that surprised you? If so, then you should look more into how you are being perceived.

Often it is easier for us to identify someone else's strengths than it is for us to recognize our own. Friends, peers and mentors can serve as a barometer for helping to gauge your strengths if you are having difficulty pin-pointing them. Ask them to share their observations of times when you have been particularly effective; times that you shine.

Some people, after a bit of self-evaluation, feel frustrated. "My strengths aren't the right ones! I want her strengths!" If this is the case with you, don't become discouraged. Although we are wired with aptitudes for certain things, through conscious effort, we can also grow ability in areas we find lacking or desirable.

For example, optimism is something I have worked hard to cultivate in my life. I have always felt that being optimistic is an important characteristic, but I had very few role models in my youth who demonstrated it, and even fewer experiences to make the case for it. Yet, inside my gut I have always longed to see the bright side of things, to know that possibilities exist beyond the often difficult reality within which I was living.

Early in my college career as a psychology major, I found literature, grounded in science, by Martin Seligman and others that corroborated my hunch about the importance of optimism. I started reading books about optimism specifically, and then about the mind, and then about the impact of emotions on performance. I learned that optimism could be increased through mental re-framing exercises. To support my efforts, I sought out friends and mentors who were optimistic and listened to them talk.

I reflected on their choices and on people's corresponding response to them, which were almost always affirmative, then mimicked their language. I did this for many years, and still do quite often. My point, of course, is that once you identify the key ingredients you want to be included in the recipe for "you," you can grow in areas that you may be naturally lacking in the desired quantity.

Unleash the Strengths of Your Team

How do you tap into the strengths of your team? Great leaders understand that the key to motivating others is to create an environment that encourages and rewards the use of individuals' talents and interests. To truly leverage the strengths of your team, build on these three things:

1. **Natural Talents and Interests**

   Find out what each member of your team likes and feels she/he is good at doing. How? Listen to them talk about how them spend discretionary time. Ask, "Without changing the whole of your job, if you could shift the amount of time you do certain tasks over others— what would you like to spend more time doing?"

2. Challenging Tasks

This is where flow comes into play. Flow is the energy at the intersection of a person's skill level and the degree of challenge associated with a given task. This means, of course, that you will need to pay close attention and ask questions. Once you have a sense that a team member is outgrowing a particular function, find ways to increase the challenge a bit. Perhaps you can add a new dimension, expand the responsibility or visibility, or ask her for input about how she would like to be more fully utilized given her growing skill set.

3. Building Self-Assurance

One of the most popular models of motivation is called Expectancy Theory, first introduced by Victor Vroom in 1964. Expectancy is the belief that a person's effort will result in attainment of desired performance goals. It is usually based on an individual's past experience, self-efficacy, and the perceived difficulty of the performance standard or goal. Self-efficacy is the person's belief about their ability to successfully perform a particular behavior.

Here's the important message for leaders related to expectancy—you have a huge role to play in whether or not a person believes that she is capable of performing a task or achieving a goal. I don't mean a fist bump and "you can do it." Try, instead, reminding her about a time in the past when she's overcome what seemed like an insurmountable obstacle, then help her connect to the benefits associated with making the effort. The key ingredient is helping the person remember the feeling associated with accomplishment associated with effort exerted toward performance of something new. This positive feeling creates the "broaden and build effect" mentioned in Strategy #5: Set a Positive Tone; broadening one's mind to possibilities and building confidence in one's ability to be successful even in the face of uncertainty.

"And what about weaknesses?" you may be asking. How do effective leaders deal with weaknesses in team members? Well, first, a disclaimer: I don't care much for focusing on weaknesses so I won't spend much time on it here. Weaknesses aren't a platform on which to build anything of substance. In the spirit, though, of minimizing weaknesses lest they get in the way, here are a few strategies for managing them:

Strategy 1: Separate skills or knowledge from talent. If the issue is skill or knowledge, disciplined attention (training, coaching) may be helpful.

Strategy 2: Find a partner. Peer-to-peer learning can be a powerful way to stay focused on overcoming something that seems too daunting to face alone.

Strategy 3: Think Sasha Fierce. You know her, right? She's Beyoncé's alter ego. Beyoncé's is a naturally shy person, yet her art and passion are as a performer. So she uses a technique that many great performers and athletes have used for years—visualization. First, she created a persona that has strength in a critical area—stage presence. She thought to herself, "What would this person, with fierce stage presence, do in front of an audience of thousands?" "What would this person with fierce stage presence wear?" "How would this person dance, and talk, and look at her adoring fans?" Finally, "What would be the appropriate name for this person?" Well, Sasha Fierce, of course! Beyoncé brilliantly created a persona who possesses huge degrees of strength where she, herself, may have perceived a weakness. Then, when it's time to perform, Beyoncé astutely and wholly becomes Sasha Fierce (and Beyoncé still gets all the credit).

Try using visualization to help your team member define and step into a "role" that is capable of performing the task at hand. Sometimes simple things like "What would a successful project plan look like—the finished product? Describe the planning process and communication that would lead to the creation of the finished product you just described? What role would you ideally play in this process and the associated communication?"

Strategy 4: Remove the weakness from the equation. If all else fails, you may need to rearrange your team member's work portfolio so that his/her weaknesses are no longer an issue. You may remove certain projects from her plate, re-evaluate performance metrics or re-assign her altogether. Just remember, there's a reason she's on your team in the first place. Think about her assets, real and potential contributions, before making sweeping judgments. Open communication is always the best first step.

Strategy 8:
Give Feedback Positively and Constructively

One of the often agonizing responsibilities of leaders is to give feedback on a performance issue requiring behavioral change. Effective managers realize that while this type of feedback may be uncomfortable, it is necessary to ensure that employees have timely information that allows immediate behavioral modification. Feedback is, when done well, given in the service of the employee, the relationship and the organization.

One of a leader's responsibilities is to help her/his employees to be effective and successful. This means providing training, support, resources, and feedback about performance issues that are getting in the way of an employee doing his or her best work. Below are some ideas of things to keep in mind when structuring feedback.

- It must be given *soon after the behavior or event occurs*. Don't wait until a behavior becomes a pattern to discuss it.

- It must *describe precisely what occurred*, with enough specificity for the person to have no trouble recalling the behavior or incident.

- It should be *limited to one issue at a time*. People are more likely to become defensive if a list is presented rather than just addressing a particular issue or behavior.

- Language must be *non-evaluative* when delivering the message. Do not ascribe attributes, motives, attitudes, or intentions.

- Give feedback only related to the *useful, actionable information*. If a person has no control over the behavior, it may not be appropriate to give feedback about it.

- Feedback should establish an opportunity for growth and/or change. *Focus on the future desired state* to underscore your ongoing investment in the relationship.

Before talking with the other person, reflect on a particular situation on which you'd like to focus. Make sure that the situation meets the above criteria. Once you have a clear understanding of the behavior about which you want to give feedback, script your opening statements to the other person.

Example: *Jenny, I observed that you came in to work today at 9:15 am, yesterday at 9:20 am, and last Tuesday at 10:15 am and you are scheduled to begin your shift at 9:00 am. I'd like to talk with you about it.*

Example: *Jonathon, yesterday when we were in the departmental meeting and just as we were beginning to discuss the new service desk policy, you packed your belongings, left the room, and the door slammed behind you. I would like to know what happened.*

You do not need to come to closure or "fix" the behavior in the opening statement. This is meant to open the conversation. Once you have invited the other person's response, listen—drop your agenda and just listen. A conversation should ensue. Allow and encourage it, because this is the time that you 1) learn more about your colleague, which will help your relationship over time, and 2) invite the other person to offer suggestions about alternative behaviors in the future. Ownership of the problem-solving process is your goal; this is the foundation of accountability.

As your conversation comes to a close, make sure that you summarize the major points raised during the discussion including the agreed upon new behaviors. Close with a plan for follow up. If appropriate, send an email message after the meeting with a list of agreed upon future behaviors and a timeline. This will be useful if additional personnel action is required.

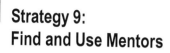

Strategy 9:
Find and Use Mentors

dentity is a combination of who I believe I am and who I am believed to be by others. The latter is often referred to as "reputation," "image" or "brand." In casual conversation on this topic, many people with whom I have spoken believe that their identity is purely, or at least largely, self-informed. It's a compilation of nature and nurture and the wide range of experiences one has had to date.

I believe that's certainly a part of the equation, but the power of others' perceptions cannot be understated. For example, I have worked with many executives who describe themselves altogether differently than do their direct reports, or—with often more pronounced differences—people several levels below them on the organizational chart. As a consultant, I am often called into organizations specifically to deal with this gap in perception; or more importantly, the repercussions that occur within the organization because this gap exists.

The Center for Creative Leadership assessed executives' self-perception and those held by others. They found a 1: .321 correlation between how executives view their behavior and how others view the same behavior. This means that 66 percent of the time executives are out of sync with their followers about how their behaviors are being perceived.

What are the consequences of not having an accurate understanding of how you are perceived? For starters, the existence of a gap of this significance is a clear signal that you are not receiving honest feedback. It is not unusual for executives to lack authentic feedback. They are often in peerless situations where the imbalance of power makes it difficult for people to share honest, sometime critical, information about behaviors for fear of retribution. Remember "The Naked Emperor"?

Even executives who invite feedback or have little or no history of retribution against employees suffer from ingrained organizational norms related to communicating with one's boss. Another consequence of not having ongoing feedback is that one becomes susceptible to over-use of those behaviors that led to one's current level of success. At face value, repeating the behaviors that have led to one's current level of success seems like an obviously sound strategy. However, it does not take into account the specific conditions under which those behaviors worked well and acknowledge that those conditions have likely changed over time. I see examples of this most often in people moving from manager to administrator level or from administrator to chief executive level. The behaviors of a top-performing manager—attention to detail, deep technical knowledge, operational excellence—are not the same as those of a top-performing administrator—strategic focus, broad knowledge base, and pattern analysis (ability to make connections between seemingly disparate pieces of environmental data).

Tips for Gaining Personal Insight

Intentionality requires self-awareness. When I practice yoga I lock eyes with my reflection in the mirror, focusing on the intricacies of each pose. With all of my best intention, though, my instructor will have perspective that I do not, and that can help me make needed adjustments. All perfect practice requires instruction and feedback. Minor corrections made soon avoid what could become a career derailer over time.

Outlined below are a few suggestions for gaining more insight about yourself and how you are perceived by others.

1. **For young professionals who want to get to the next level: Find a leadership coach.**

Select a coach who matches where you are professionally and with whom you can communicate well. Make sure that the coach understands your needs. Do you need problem-solving support for issues like managing employees' performance? Or supporting your work-life integration needs? Do you need someone to facilitate the exploration of your next step and long-term career options? Or are you looking for someone to help you map your transition into an executive position? In any of these cases, an outside party whose job it is to help you think methodically through options and support you in the decision making process is an incredibly helpful resource.

2. **For seasoned professionals who want to sharpen your edge and build organizational capacity: Commit to ongoing formal and informal assessment.**

Successful people are reflective. I know, I know. There are plenty of examples of people who are not reflective, not at all in touch with themselves and how they are perceived by others, and yet are in positions of leadership. This is true. Yet there are just as many recent cases of people like this who have fallen from grace—losing their careers, their fortunes, their credibility. Remember, the higher up you go in the formal leadership ranks, the more important it is to truly commit to self-betterment, making small adjustments along the way that will keep you from experiencing a major career setback. Today, 360 degree assessments are increasingly common for executive leaders' performance evaluation. With that said, I strongly discourage one's first exposure to a 360 degree assessment come through a performance review process. Rather, 360 degree assessments are most helpful as developmental tools, so seek out an opportunity through your boss or the Human Resources office to participate in a 360 degree review as part of a leadership experience or a succession planning effort. You will use the same type of instrument so popularly used as a performance tool for senior leaders, but within the confines of a learning experience that allows you to receive feedback, internalize it, and then work to make needed changes. This approach also means that you are taking control of your perception, and reinforces your reputation as a credible leader who is willing to walk the walk.

3. **For someone who is looking to develop a particular skill set: Get a coach or take a class. Do something structured that helps you keep your focus, allows you to have feedback on performance and progress, and holds you accountable for follow through.**

Soliciting Feedback

The most important thing I can say about feedback is this: embrace it. If the phrase "perception is reality" is indeed correct, it's worth the personal effort to seek feedback regularly and act on it. Relatively minor course-corrections in behavior keep the perception gap small and manageable—decreasing the probability of being blindsided.

Remember the 6:1 ratio? For every time you give someone corrective feedback, you should have six times provided that same person feedback about how her/his behaviors were helpful and should be repeated. The same is true for receiving feedback. Find out about the areas in which you are doing well.

These are important for you to know because it helps you clarify and own your strengths. Here's another thing about feedback, if you don't want it and won't be influenced by it, don't ask for it.

Feedback is most effectively given and received if both parties understand the motivation behind the request and believe that information is being shared in the best interest of the soliciting party. As the recipient, I must believe that honest feedback is going to give me helpful insight that I would not otherwise have access to and that will help me make useful behavioral decisions, about repeating certain behaviors or making changes. If I am not willing to change my behavior, I should not ask for feedback. Inviting feedback creates an expectation on the part of the person giving the feedback. If that expectation isn't met, she/he will likely not be willing to honor future requests of the solicitor.

My second piece of advice related to soliciting feedback is to focus the invitation. It's difficult to know where to begin when asking for feedback. "Do you have anything you'd like to share with me?" "Are there things I'm doing about which you'd like to give me feedback?" These are not quite specific enough questions. While they are open-ended and invite commentary on any number of behaviors, it's more helpful to focus the inquiry.

It's also helpful to remember that it's difficult for people to give feedback about you, as a person. Particularly if a solid and positive relationship exists, people are hesitant to share criticisms about what may be perceived as one's personality or character. Instead, focus on behaviors and/or a situation that is bound by a focused period of time. "I'd like to hear your thoughts about what went well at today's Cabinet meeting and what might be done to encourage higher levels of contribution from everyone." "It seems to me that we're having some difficulty seeing eye-to-eye on how to proceed with the next phase of our plan. I think we share a vision of where we would ultimately like to go but would like to get your input about how we might approach this initiative differently, to get us on the same page."

4. For Everyone: Find a Mentor. Find Several Mentors.

Within a mentoring relationship, giving feedback needs to be couched as one element of a multi-faceted and constructive relationship. Let us explore mentoring relationships here.

Mentors…and Anti-Mentors

Mentoring is key for leadership development, for young people who are at the early stages of crafting their identity, for managers who are looking for models to help shape, articulate and execute against the backdrop of a vision, and for people who are more seasoned in their lives and careers and understand the significance of giving back as integrally connected to creating a legacy.

Definitions:

Mentor:
Someone who 1) has experience-based wisdom in a particular area and 2) actively invests in the development of another person.

Protégé:
A person seeking growth in a particular area of her/his personal and/or professional life and is committed to learning from and with a person possessing experience-based wisdom.

Anti-Mentor:
Someone who actively subjugates others and/or models undesirable behaviors.

Mentoring Relationship Roles

In establishing and maintaining a solid mentoring relationship, certain conditions must be met. Both need to share enough to establish rapport, agree to level of confidentiality and expectations regarding communication style and frequency. Whether concentrated for a short period of time or one that will span for a longer duration, this relationship must include an explicit commitment to care for and respect each other.

Sometimes protégés approach a mentor with a specific "ask" in mind. For example, one request I typically hear from mid-level managers is, "I'd like a mentor who can teach me about budgeting." This desire is perfectly acceptable for a more junior person, and a helpful mentor may, in that instance, recommend a budgeting course or set aside time to walk through budgeting spreadsheets used by their company or in a particular department.

Coming from a mid-level manager, however, the request to learn more about budgeting might be considered differently. The mentor's role is to listen to what the protégé is saying but through the lenses of her/his experience. A helpful mentor may say in response to the aforementioned request, "Given your senior leadership aspirations, what I think would be more helpful for you is to learn about the budgeting and resource allocation process—the cycle, the politics, how to position yourself to get a seat at the decision-making table."

Protégé/ Mentor Roles

Protégé	Mentor
Reflects on needs and defines the scope of the relationship	Creates learning experiences and exchanges that respond to protégés needs
Describes goals	Listens and uses personal experience and insight to appropriately challenge the scope of protégé's goals.
Reflects on needs	Matches personal experience and resource base with need needs of protégé.
Actively listens	Actively listens
Asks for feedback	Asks for feedback

Find mentors that represent the strongest and most significant assets— those three to five core strengths upon which you have potential to build and position yourself for influence. I encourage you to use mentors to help extend portions of yourself that are already strong, rather than focusing on turning weaknesses into strengths. There are mountains of research that show that you will get a much higher return on investment if you focus on leveraging that for which you are already have a predisposition and enjoy.

Mentors should exude the characteristics that you already have and have the capacity to help you figure out how best to harness their potential. Surround yourself with people who are positive and upbeat, are where you want to be, and doing the things that you want to do. Seek out the company of people who are making things happen. Put yourself into an environment that exposes you through peer-pressure to be better than you currently are—better, stronger, faster.

Reflect back to the leadership characteristics you found most effective in the "Branding" section. Now, think about how those characteristics resonate with your own strengths and potential strengths. Next step, connect to your personal values. Do the characteristics exuded by your mentors-to-be reflect their values and your own? For example, your mentor may be a high-earning sales representative; an attractive and desirable outcome for you. On the other hand, she may have had to forego having a family, something you desire. Or the C-Suite executive you so admire may have international business trips three times a month during which he is wined and dined. But he is overweight and his stress levels make you concerned for his long-term well-being. I am not asking you to put yourself in the position of judging other's reality. I am encouraging you, though, to think holistically about what you want to create for yourself, consistently able to answer your own conscious about the "why".

If creating an intentional leadership practice is your goal, I encourage you to seek mentors who have disciplined intellectual, exercise, family and social habits and robust spiritual lives that keep them energized and whole. Find people who read as much as you wish you read, who have the kinds of quality relationships with their children that you wish you had, who exercise as much as you wish you would exercise, who are as productive as you wish you were. Surround yourself with people like this and you will be anchoring yourself to a positive and aspirational peer group.

As I look back over my mentoring relationships to identify the common threads, I would say that each of my great mentors has demonstrated similar qualities. They:

- Focused on my needs;

- Did not try to change me into her/him;

- Did not tell me what to do, but guided me through difficult decisions I had to make;

- Allowed me to fail, but helped me recover quickly and learn from it; and

- Let me shine.

When I talk to groups and ask them to share the qualities of great mentors they have had, their list is very similar to my own. Interestingly and without fail, in each of those instances people have also shared examples of how the desire to *not* be like a particular person has shaped them. These people are potential role models, friends or teachers or bosses, who are unkind to others and behave in ways that are unflattering. I don't mean unflattering in a "that dress makes you look fat" kind of way.

The terms "mentors" and "anti-mentors" are not meant to imply that within a particular person there is either all goodness and light or selfishness and mayhem. We bring our humanity to all that we do, personally and professionally. Each of us has strong points and weaker ones. Mentors are not perfect people. And anti-mentors are not evil—they're just not necessarily people you want to model your life after or that you want to help you (or would likely be interested in helping you) find a path, or hone a skill.

Admittedly, we have all been grateful for little slips made by exemplary people; it helps us recognize that they are human too. There's a certain release on the internal pressure gauge that makes us feel less than adequate as compared to those high achievers. But there is no excuse for poor management practices that create toxic work environments or interpersonal relationships that tear down rather than build us up. Think about your own life and experiences. How many mentors have shaped you and how have they helped you become the person you are today? How many anti-mentors have influenced you and what effect have they had on you?

Sometimes the desire to find a mentor and become more like them has led to our becoming overly dependent or emulative in a way that causes you to lose your authentic voice. This can be a major mistake in achieving your goals. Admiration should not lead to literally following in someone else's footsteps. Being a carbon copy of a peer or predecessor does not produce success; embracing your own uniqueness is what wins the day.

Instead of trying to follow another person's path, blaze your own trail based on your own skills, strengths and abilities. These are the qualities that will set you apart in the marketplace. Do not interpret this advice as diminishing the importance of mentors. They are essential and have a lifetime of lessons and experiences worth repeating and avoiding. Mentors can provide invaluable feedback and open doors to networks. However, it is up to you to seize these opportunities. What will make you memorable is your personal brand, not the fact that you were introduced by or were the guest of your mentor.

So what are some techniques for making a strong and lasting impression? Before attending an event with your mentor, ask her/him to give you information that allows you to do a bit of research in advance. Look at pictures online from last year's event—what are people wearing? Ask the name(s) of the hosts or hosting organizations, then get to know a bit about them. Prepare to be introduced to the host and have something personal to say, something that shows that you did your homework. Did you attend college in the same state? Do you have the same undergraduate degree? Did you sister-in-law used to work for the hosting company? Find a connection, and share it. Striking up a conversation with a person about himself and what he does demonstrates an interest in the other person, knowledge of his work and industry. It also shows that you understand the importance of preparation; sets you apart as a person who takes seriously the opportunities given to you and are eager to be considered a colleague or new friend.

At the end of the event, follow up with the people you met and from whom you collected business cards. Send a LinkedIn invitation or a short yet personalized email, sharing your contact information. Send a hand-written "thank you" card to the host, if possible. Again, the intention is to make sure that you are in the driver's seat when it comes to sharing your brand with new acquaintances, and are not relegated to merely being your mentor's sidekick. This reflects well on you and on your mentor.

Strategy 10:
Design and Commit to a Disciplined Practice

This strategy is all about mapping your next steps, making a personal commitment, and then following through day-in and day-out with purpose and intention. You, of course, are in charge of establishing a vision, defining the measure of your success. If you did as I encourage, though, and anchored highly to a vision that is audacious, it will take a lot of disciplined effort to achieve. No worries, highly anchored, compelling visions will benefit from the eustress they create.

Remember that your intentional leadership path will need more structure than can be provided by creative energy alone. So let's circle back now to vision, and tie together the various threads of your intentional path. Using the **Values to Vision: Putting Your Leadership Goals in Context** worksheet provided on the following page, take some time to reflect on your whole self.

Exercise:

1. Identify your top five values in action—those values that more than others influence your decisions and behaviors on a day-to-day basis. This is difficult. You will likely have many more than five values that immediately come to mind. Force yourself to choose the top five that actually determine your behavior.

2. Consistent with the values that you identified in the previous step, what are some of your specific career goals? Do not limit yourself to thinking only of your career path or job options as you have considered them to date. Really force yourself to think about work that is intentionally connected to your values in action.
How do those goals reflect your values? Where are they out of sync?

3. Consider the aspects that are described in the outer ring of the graphic—your family, geographic location and preferences, health and finances. Describe your aspiration in each of these areas, feeling free to add other areas

that are important to you. Again, there is no need to stay within the realm of "current reality" for this exercise. Describe your goals, particularly as they reflect and grow out of your values in action.

4. After making notes in each of the three arenas, look at the whole worksheet. What are your initial observations? Now, share your goals and insights with a mentor or trusted friend. Discuss tensions, gaps or happy surprises.

Values to Vision: Putting Your Leadership Goals in Context

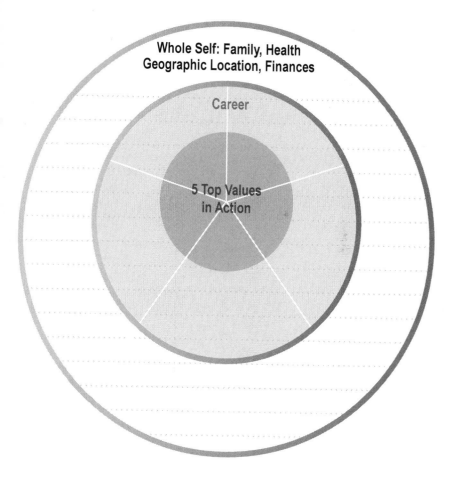

Whole Self: Family, Health
Geographic Location, Finances

Career

5 Top Values
in Action

The final step in your putting into place your intentional practice is concretizing your goals and identifying exactly what is needed to help you achieve them. Once you have completed the Values to Vision exercise and processed your responses with a trusted advisor, complete the **Begin Your Perfect Practice** worksheet. This format breaks your leadership practice into specific areas of focus, for a more disciplined approach to managing change and measuring performance over time.

Begin Your Perfect Practice Worksheet

Goals	Knowledge Needed	Skills Needed	Mindset Change	Behavior Change

Now you have it, ten easy strategies to consider and, hopefully, integrate into your intentional leadership practice. There are of course a plethora of additional resources that I encourage you to seek out, including many of the sources cited in this book. The most important thing is that you build intentionality, from the outset, into your holistic approach and then that you create habits that allow you to practice and seek ongoing feedback.

I wish you well. Please feel free to reach out to me or any of the members of my team for additional information, coaching or tips. I would also love to hear about your practice and achievements. Share your success stories with me through Twitter, @DeEttaMJones, or my blog www.DeEttaJones.com.

Namaste.

34742891R00037

Made in the USA
Lexington, KY
27 March 2019